T0196409

YOU ARE ALWAYS GOOD TO GO

AMR MUNEER DAHAB

author**HOUSE**®

AuthorHouse™
1663 Liberty Drive
Bloomington, IN 47403
www.authorhouse.com
Phone: 833-262-8899

Published by AuthorHouse 02/25/2021

ISBN: 978-1-6655-1822-2 (sc)
ISBN: 978-1-6655-1821-5 (e)

To those who feel hesitant to go and have the potential; to those who are reluctant to go and need to find the potential

CONTENTS

PREFACE

My previous book, *Facing Troublemakers,* was not only an encouragement to write *You Are Always Good to Go*; it basically inspired it. After *Facing Troublemakers,* I found that it is exciting to encourage readers, emphasizing that confronting their opponents is not the only thing that could be done better than they believe, but it is possible to handle life as a whole far better than commonly assumed.

You Are Always Good to Go attempts to ensure that there is always something positive you can do even in the toughest times, rather than just get annoyed or sit helplessly.

I hope you will get inspired to go on positively despite circumstances that commonly look difficult and frustrating. You will realize that there are easy, positive actions to do while you are waiting, hesitant, afraid, or even taking a break.

YOU ARE ALWAYS GOOD TO DO SOMETHING

1

👍 The question is not whether to go or stay. It is rather, *Where should I go and how?*

👍 Deeply believe in your present; you are always the best current version of yourself.

👍 Encouraging supporters are sources of hope; frustrating people should be a source of challenge and determination.

👍 Perfection is impossible; it is always about the acceptable level of imperfection.

👍 Compare yourself to yesterday's version; feel grateful for improvement and for opportunities to have learned lessons.

👍 Take care of your pride along the way; never let anyone violate it, and do not overestimate it.

👍 You are always good to do something: to go, to wait, to have a break. Just be careful in selecting the proper action, and make sure you are most positive about that action.

👍 To discover your strength, avoid gazing too much at others and take a deep look inside yourself.

👍 Do not feel afraid to discover your weaknesses in order to address and handle these weaknesses, and do not let them frustrate you.

👍 Do not let the presence of others affect your decision to go somewhere. We cannot eliminate people who are in our way in life, so how can we imagine eliminating them from their ways?

👍 Always believe that tomorrow you could do better and yesterday you could not have done better.

👍 Complimentary words from people are good sources for encouragement, and their criticism has an unavoidable negative impact in one way or another. However, do not let your level of self-esteem be determined by others.

👍 It is never that you are bad; it is always that you could get better.

👍 Sometimes, all you need to do to feel better is to reevaluate your current status.

👍 If assessing your situation reveals hidden undesired issues, you should not let yourself feel worse; be grateful that you have learned what you must tackle and improve.

👍 You are the one who knows better how far you are good. However, consider trustworthy opinions from people around you.

TO GO WITH TIME

2

👍 It is never too late; you can still do it, mostly in a different way.

👍 If you can do it now, why delay it? Make sure you have solid justifications before deciding to delay anything.

👍 When you find yourself lacking new goals, think about repeating some old ideas—not necessarily in every detail, and preferably with a new approach.

👍 It is good to ask, *When can I do it*? It is better to think, *What can I do now?*

👍 A precise plan is necessary for any journey. However, that does not necessitate observing a stopwatch continuously; frequent measurements of blood pressure might lead unconsciously to increasing it.

👍 Do not rush. With well-prepared plans, arriving before the scheduled time will not necessarily be an added value.

👍 When you arrive before the planned time anyway, you could start the next journey earlier if that does not disturb consequent commitments. Alternatively, you may finalize unfinished minor items on your list of pending tasks.

👍 Even though time is an essential part of planning any journey, that does not always mean the faster, the better.

👍 Contrary to what we might tend to believe, journeys without exact durations are often the most difficult. Life is the biggest example.

👍 Time is not money; avoid underestimating time.

👍 It is never late, and the lesson learned is that next time you should arrive on time.

👍 There is always something to do; your relaxation should be part of your agenda, not something you do when you cannot find anything else to do.

👍 When you do not find anything to do, that does not mean there is nothing to do. You just cannot see what is waiting for you to accomplish.

👍 While you are trying to discover your hidden missions, you could lend your hand to those overwhelmed with missions. It is not always just to assist them finishing something; they might only be in need of being refueled with positive energy.

👍 Time is generous as much as you use it.

👍 The time allocated determines the way you should carry out and finish the task. Make sure that you accurately estimate the project's duration to allow the work to fit into the time you have available.

👍 The same duration in different situations could be enough to complete one, two, or plenty of tasks. You just need to focus on what to sacrifice: unnecessary details, your rest time, the energy needed to work faster, and so on.

IT IS NEVER A WAR

3

👍 It is more practical and helpful to handle difficult situations as a game rather than a battle. You will be more serene and might even enjoy such situations.

👍 Even in the middle of a war, before thinking of using illegal weapons, make sure that you have effectively utilized any legal weapons at your disposal.

👍 Using illegal weapons in a war will not necessarily give you an advantage over your enemy. It could complicate your position and lead to disastrous consequences.

👍 In disputes, do not in your rush get excited and use the term "weapons"; they are just "tools", and by using them intelligently, you could achieve better results than a soldier could do using weapons in a real battle.

👍 When voices rise inside you during a critical situation about the necessity of using illegal means, do not rush to accept them. This is most likely a sign of weakness or confusion rather than exceptional circumstances calling for the violation of basic principles.

👍 There are no good tools or bad tools. It is all about selecting the right tool at the right time and using it wisely.

👍 Attempting to use illegal tools in any kind of dispute is of course unethical. Quite often it looks much more like a lazy act to find a shortcut to end the dispute rather than being a deliberate act to bypass ethics.

👍 Declaring war in normal daily conflicts, or rushing to accept others' declarations of war, is mostly a sign of agitation that reveals the devil inside you. Do your best to avoid satisfying that deceitfully perilous tendency.

👍 When others insist on behaving toward you as if at war, maintain your calm—but it is important to show them that you are completely ready for war.

👍 You are OK as long as you are not captured; but remember: confinement is not only behind bars.

👍 Illegal means are not magic tools you use when you are desperate to guarantee reaching your goals. They have harmful effects on you and the opponent in equal measure. And they are not necessarily less damaging to the initiator.

👍 People tending to use illegal means are not necessarily smart. Nevertheless, you should be more alert with them.

👍 Quite often it looks to be a fine line between what is legal and what is illegal. We should strive to make borders clearer rather than utilizing the gray area for our interests.

TO GO WITH ETHICS

4

👍 Ethics do not keep you from moving positively. Stubbornness in interpreting ethics does.

👍 We often act and then try to justify our behaviors to suit our interpretations of ethics.

👍 When we find no escape from admitting that we have been pragmatic in our behavior, we subsequently tend to have an amazing ability to forget.

👍 Our material interests are the most dangerous competitors of our desire to be ethical.

👍 Critical times are the real test of ethics. Who would resist the temptation to stick to ethical approaches when it costs him no loss?

👍 The most pragmatic actors do not declare they are bypassing ethics; they just invent their own ethical definitions.

👍 Power has a magical influence to convince its audience that it is ethical whatever it does.

👍 You must get rid of your weaknesses to convince others of the value of your ethics.

👍 Ethics should not be a choice, but it is definitely a challenge.

👍 You should not bargain away your principles at any cost; just be flexible when expressing these principles in front of others, especially those who are or will be negatively affected by them.

👍 Your real test of adherence to ethics comes only during tough times.

👍 Easy times are luxurious tests of our ethical tendencies.

👍 Ethics by definition is a continuous challenge. Reevaluation is a continuous need.

👍 Ethics will not primarily eliminate barriers from your path. Rather, ethics are the necessary humps that will slow you down as you speed toward your destination.

👍 The choice to ignore ethics completely will not make the journey as easy as you might imagine. While some difficulties will disappear when ignoring ethics, other tough challenges will certainly rise up in turn.

👍 Ignoring a tough ethical challenge on your way will give you the impression that you have almost reached your destination. Enjoy that feeling while it lasts, but remember: it is not a fact.

Challenges stop only after reaching your destination, and not even just a few steps before that.

👍 Ethics are never the reason for not reaching your destination. It is all about the approach you use to handle your ethics.

👍 When you think about bypassing ethics, justifications look unlimited. Work hard and don't get excused.

👍 Good companions along the way are important; take care of them. It is not wise to tire them out with the consequences of your principles.

TO GO WITH PRIDE

5

👍 Pride is a deep feeling you do not need to insist on showing it every step of the way.

👍 Never let your pride take the lead.

👍 The true test of the poise of your pride lies in not hesitating to admit your mistakes in the middle of a confrontation.

👍 Your pride is absolutely precious; instead of defending it from real and imagined encroachments, avoid engaging it in every battle along the way.

👍 You are responsible for the image and limits of your pride. Do not let others push you into fabricated battles to defend it.

👍 Let the wounds of your pride heal quickly; they get dramatically worse and become more difficult to control if you do not give them enough attention.

👍 Everyone has his or her own way of defining and expressing pride. Beware of those who are good at hiding their big ego.

👍 By dealing wisely with your pride during different situations, you can increase your gains. Excessive stubbornness hurts your pride.

👍 Your test of pride gets harder when you discover your mistake late on the road of intense disagreement.

👍 Your pride is affirmative when it inspires others and not just satisfies yourself.

TO GO WITH FEAR

6

👍 Your fear deserves better than avoidance; face it.

👍 You cannot know how strong you are unless you face your fears.

👍 Rather than having physical existence, our fears tend to be exaggerated imaginings and even delusions.

👍 Slight fear sometimes acts as a catalyst, expediting you to progress faster. Just beware of letting fear grow stronger.

👍 You cannot be absolutely fearless, but you must face your fears to ensure that you are not afraid of illusions.

👍 Your fears do not only constitute your boundaries. They can push you behind your abilities.

👍 We do not fear real danger as much as we are afraid of fear itself.

👍 Do not trust nonaggression treaties with fear. Make sure that you have defeated it.

👍 People you are afraid of could be afraid of you. However, remember it is not an intimidation match. Just trust yourself and proceed on your way.

👍 When you dare to overcome your fears, it not only helps you advance on the road but also opens new horizons to you.

👍 Fear is contagious and spreads rapidly. If you surrender to it on one road, it will appear to you on other roads.

👍 It is good to laugh at your old fears. Let that remind you how easily your current fears will pass in time.

👍 When others speak about their fears, instead of being affected by their stories, try to inspire them to be courageous. That is what you and others need regardless of their intentions and your initial spontaneous reactions.

👍 A brave heart desperately needs a smart and wise mind.

TO GO WITH HESITATION

7

👍 When you are not certain about two or more options, remember that you might find the solution outside these options.

👍 It is good to finalize your decisions well before the deadline you have set. Your options become fewer and making decisions turn out to be harder with the rhythm of the countdown.

👍 Not every case of uncertainty should push you to worry. Hesitation requires attention when it lasts for a long time or frequently recurs.

👍 It is more effective to seek advice subsequent to thinking intensely about the subject, not immediately after you begin to hesitate making your decision about available and possible choices.

👍 Rushing to seek advice when hesitant to make a decision may provide more options that further confuse you. Slow down, and think carefully about what you really need advice on.

👍 It is OK to change your mind after making a decision, but be careful if you were already hesitant before that decision.

👍 When you are hesitant, remember that no decision is absolutely right. Do not be too afraid of mistakes if everything is relative.

👍 Knowing what you truly want is not always an advantage. When you find yourself getting more impulsive than usual, you sometimes need to reconsider your decision.

👍 Feeling overconfident could be more harmful than being hesitant. You tend to seek advice when hesitant. But when overconfident, you lack the sensors necessary to alert you of the need to stop or at least slow down.

👍 If 100 percent is perfection, then 120 percent is probably imperfection.

TO GO WITH LUCK

8

👍 Luck is not something that you wait for; just go and find it somewhere on your way.

👍 Maintaining positive energy and looking at the bright side of things lets you feel that you are always lucky.

👍 Luck is an absolute belief. Believe in it and you get it.

👍 It is a fallacy to determine that someone is luckier and more pleased than another unless you know what both achieved out of what both had dreamed. Yet satisfaction is an essential nonmeasurable factor.

👍 Luck is not a magic wand. It just gives a satisfactory explanation to unintelligible successes.

👍 Luck looks like a happy ending of a story rather than the means leading to that happy end.

👍 Instead of waiting for luck to make you happy, be happy in order to get lucky.

👍 It is rare—and more likely impossible—for luck to knock on your door if you are reluctant to go out.

👍 Always search for your good luck within what happened, and you will find it.

TO GO WITH FAITH

9

👍 Your beliefs will not let you down. But remember: you are not supposed to dictate your expectations to those beliefs.

👍 Believe and do not wait and see. Rather, work and see.

👍 The most harmful impurities to the fuel of faith's power are doubts.

👍 The rewards of faith come slowly but last a long time.

👍 The most accurate measure of your depth of faith is your patience in getting through tough times, even more than how grateful you feel in hours of relief.

👍 Faith deepens the fleeting pleasure of relief.

👍 Faith grows and deepens over time. It is exceptional to be deeply faithful since a young age.

👍 Face this fact, admit it, and continuously attempt to comply with its content: Faith needs frequent renewal.

👍 The test of true faith, and its pleasure at the same time, is that it is something you keep paying for with a great reward that will be long awaited but will definitely come.

👍 You do not need a guide to tell you about genuinely faithful believers. You will be attracted to them spontaneously.

COMPARISONS ON THE WAY

10

👍 Comparisons with others are useless when they do not push you toward enhancement. And they can be dangerous when they lead you to frustration.

👍 Comparison is one way of learning. To pass the exam, avoid copying.

👍 You will not feel happy if others compared themselves to you and just felt happy. They should be inspired by that comparison and get busy.

👍 In general, spontaneous comparisons tend to be more fruitful than intended ones.

👍 There are no absolute comparisons. Be specific in determining the area of comparison, and be objective in the judgment.

👍 It seems safer to compare others to others than to compare others to yourself. That is not necessarily accurate. You still need to be specific and objective.

👍 Avoid exaggerating comparisons. Remember that the alerting question in this regard is, "How severely do I compare?" rather than, "How often do I compare?"

👍 Focus on inspiring others after they compare themselves to you rather than just leaving them to feel jealous.

👍 Slight jealousy is normal after comparing yourself to someone having more admirable qualities in certain areas. But make sure to move quickly toward practical steps to enhance your actions.

👍 Comparisons should not be your primary tools for development. You must continuously set and update benchmarks considering your current achievements and future potential.

👍 It is not that you cannot avoid comparisons, you should not avoid comparisons.

👍 If you aim to be special, you need to know exactly how others look and act.

👍 Being special demands that you accept the fact that others might exceed you in areas of comparison. Uniqueness is something rarely relevant to any sort of quantities.

👍 Your insistence on selflessness toward others means that you want to be better off than they are through that behavior.

IT IS A SMALL WORLD; IT IS ALL YOURS **11**

👍 In today's life, remember that our way is the whole world.

👍 It always used to be a small world, and it is getting smaller. That makes almost everywhere reachable for you.

👍 Today's interconnected world increases the challenge levels and multiplies the opportunities as well.

👍 Contrary to what you might believe, if you are not doing well in your own place, it does not mean you will be worse outside your native land. Give it a serious and sincere try.

👍 In today's world, most of our paths are becoming virtual. Be careful as that might double your communication challenges.

👍 Even if you are a good communicator through virtual media, avoid overconfidence as well as an underestimation of nonphysical interaction barriers.

👍 What is seen by others as cultural barriers could be interesting challenges for you or even areas of strength.

👍 While adapting some of others' cultural approaches when dealing with them, try to express some of your own cultural attitudes that might be interesting to others. Doing so may enhance the chances of better communication.

👍 When getting into a new culture, do not overexert yourself with an all-or-nothing rule. Success probably comes step by step, and your beginner's mistakes will be justifiable. Just be careful not to repeat your mistakes.

👍 Being good at using new technology is not enough to succeed at promoting yourself or your product through Internet and electronic media. You need to be good at expressing yourself and have the required skills for what you are intending to grab people's attention.

👍 Almost the same basic principles of communication apply to all areas. Do not get distracted when new means emerge. You can learn how to use them or delegate someone to use them for you. The content always remains yours, and you should control it your way.

👍 Do not hesitate to revisit some areas of previous failures when you feel you have learned from your mistakes and you are ready to apply new approaches confidently.

YOU ARE ALWAYS GOOD TO GIVE

12

👍 Giving is a rich source of confidence and satisfaction.

👍 There is always someone in need and who will welcome your giving.

👍 Contrary to what you might think, your difficult times are the most suitable for giving. They offer you needed and deserved relief.

👍 People in need, areas of giving, and your ability to give are unlimited.

👍 Sometimes accepting a simple offer from a humble person is a kind of giving.

👍 You are giving in one way or another. Just enlarge your giving circle regarding number of people and nature of gifts.

👍 The quality of giving has nothing to do with anyone's financial status. In fact, the relationship between the nature of giving and materialistic comfort often appears to be an inverse one.

👍 To give or not to give? That is not the question. Rather, the question is what to give?

👍 Widening your nature of giving enables you to continue to give with ease and pleasure.

👍 Seek giving inspiration within those who seem to have less than you do.

👍 It is good to give any of what you can. It is better, however, to give when possible what others need most.

👍 Do not worry a lot if giving becomes an addiction for you. Just beware of the addiction of taking.

👍 Giving pays back when you do not wait for it.

👍 Volunteer work is one of the most valued kinds of giving. But you can offer a similar kind of giving, or even surpass that, when you try to achieve perfection in your regular day-to-day work.

👍 There are always times when you do not want to go out though someone is pushing you to do so on his or her behalf. If doing so does not contradict your interests or principles, do not hesitate to support the person. What you find ridiculous or boring might mean a lot to others. Being patient and helping will be paid back in one way or another.

WHOM AND WHAT TO AVOID?

13

👍 Avoid avoidance.

👍 Don't waste your time thinking how to avoid unwanted people or undesirable situations. There is always a good way to deal with a worst-case scenario.

👍 Prepare the best scenario for the worst case.

👍 Being ready and showing that you are always ready push others to initiate avoidance.

👍 You cannot completely avoid everything around you. But you can certainly control your involvement in anything.

👍 Better than obsessing about avoiding making previous mistakes, focus on seeing new opportunities even within the same previous actions.

👍 Avoid delaying.

👍 Do not let others control your progress by intentionally avoiding you. Force them to confront you or look for other alternatives, and adopt the most suitable ones.

👍 Continuously frustrating people deserve worse than avoidance. Remove them from your way.

👍 Avoid unstudied risks.

👍 Remember that life is not always packages of options. There are many experiences that you will not like but must do.

👍 When you cannot avoid a challenge, face it with a smart mind and a brave heart.

👍 Your distinguished achievements are not always what you have deliberately chosen to do.

👍 Believe in your choices and in your destiny on the same level as it is quite hard to distinguish between them.

👍 It is good to acknowledge that you have learned a lot from experiences you were forced to go through, and that you even liked some of them.

👍 Your choices are your pleasant friends. Your obligations are your tough mentors.

WHEN DO YOU NEED TO WAIT?

14

👍 When you feel hesitant, face your fears. When in doubt, think carefully, but do not delay the decision for too long.

👍 To wait and see should be your last choice for dealing with rising obstacles. However, you are still capable to reach for other destinations while observing what is happening with current obstacles.

👍 It will be a waste of time to sit idly while waiting. Reevaluate your past actions, and discover possible opportunities and alternatives so you are ready for any result.

👍 You should control the duration of your wait. Do not let others hinder you from driving at your optimal speed.

👍 If you must wait for any reason, others do not necessarily need to know that you are waiting.

👍 Finding others proceeding on their ways while you are waiting does not mean that they are ahead. They might be forgetting items to continue the journey.

👍 Although the factors that necessitate waiting are mostly out of your hands, it is always good to anticipate the length of the wait.

👍 You might accept extending the anticipated waiting period when you feel that positive outcomes are close to appearing, and you are not delaying anything outside the waiting zone.

👍 However, avoid as much as possible extending an already extended waiting period.

👍 Try to finalize pending tasks during your waiting times. But do not let that distract you from observing the task you are waiting on.

👍 When you start waiting, immediately review the originally planned time left to get to your destination. That allows you to react wisely while you are waiting and adhere to your original plan as much as possible.

DECIDING TO GIVE IT A BREAK

15

👍 Avoiding people would never help you settle situations. When you decide to step back for tactical purposes, plan your timed break carefully.

👍 A break does not mean that you should necessarily close all doors behind you. However, do not forget to keep some windows always open for fresh air.

👍 A necessary break is not an indication that you are helpless. Rather, it is a healthy stage in the journey toward your destination within any relationship.

👍 When you are in a break, it does not mean to stop thinking. Calm planning for the next step helps you to relax better and be better-prepared to face people after the break.

👍 When your opponent is hyperactive, it is important to give him or her a forced break. That is the smartest way to absorb the opponent's energy.

👍 Pushing your hyperactive opponent to a forced break from the current issue is achievable by distracting him or her with side matters.

👍 Keep your opponents confused about what you might be doing during the break. Do not overthink about what they might be doing in the same situation.

👍 An entirely different business destination could be an excellent break from your current exhausting task. You do not need literally to take a holiday.

👍 Do not wait for an annual leave or even a forced break. Let the break to clear your mind and soul be a daily habit.

👍 You are free to choose the appropriate time for your mind- and soul-clearing break throughout the day. However, it is better to adhere to a fixed time and even a defined place.

👍 When you decide during the break to end a relationship, do not just disappear. You should face the other party with your decision.

👍 Remember that breaking up is not the only action when finding things are not going as expected with the current choice. You can adopt other options simultaneously.

HOW COULD YOU BE BETTER? 16

👍 When it is about the version of yourself, rest assured that you are always good to go. Never wait for a better copy of yourself to start moving forward.

👍 Unless you are overthinking, tomorrow should bring the best copy of yourself for that day.

👍 You are better as long as you are not affected by others' underestimations as well as not overestimating yourself.

👍 You should accept fluctuations while working hard on getting better. However, the curve of your better version should be ascending in the long term.

👍 A better copy of yourself is always relative as it is judged considering continuous new challenges.

👍 It is difficult to talk about a single better copy of yourself. There are many copies of yourself depending on the fields and angles from which others happen to look at you.

👍 Actually, everyone has several versions of him- or herself at the same time.

👍 It is unwise to ignore people's opinions about you. However, it is mainly your own opinions about yourself that matter.

👍 Getting better is easier to achieve by focusing on your targets rather than just being obsessed with a better image.

👍 You will never have one better image of yourself presentable to everyone.

👍 Do not work hard to hide from people the sides of you that they do not like. However, it wise to bring other people's attention to what they most like in your personality.

👍 Normally, we tend to work on achieving better copies of ourselves in the areas others are currently concerned with.

👍 Being better starts with a genuine desire, continues with a solid will, and is achieved with a strong psychological belief.

INSPIRE OR GET INSPIRED

17

👍 Copying others' ways to the same destination does not guarantee to get you there. Verify the factors affecting your own experience, and select your way accordingly.

👍 There is always a chance to be inspired by others' journeys even if their destinations are different than yours.

👍 It is not about being right or wrong; it is your confidence that inspires others.

👍 You are strong as far as you can inspire or be inspired. Your weakness arises when you copy others or feel afraid of being deservedly inspired by their actions.

👍 Inspiration is not just a decision; it is a deep belief.

👍 Consider your previous successes as a good source to inspire yourself. But do not forget your failures as they are no less an important source of inspiration.

👍 Inspiration is a kind of a healthy infection. However, it can spread among people involved in different-natured activities.

👍 Inspiration has an easy access to people with open hearts and open minds.

👍 To make sure that you got inspired and did not just copy others, give yourself some time to think about what you genuinely admired, and then do it your own way.

👍 Becoming inspired is an unconscious behavior. However, it is better to be aware of what inspires you.

👍 Knowing what inspired you helps to inspire you further.

👍 Do not limit your chances to get inspired by focusing on those you think are better than you. Inspiration is available around you more widely than you think.

18

TOGETHER ON OUR WAYS

👍 On your way, always do it your way. And remember that others share the road with you.

👍 There is no dedicated path for anyone alone in life.

👍 On your way, there always needs to be a careful balance between insisting on passing first and giving priority for others to pass.

👍 Occasionally it might look more like a car race than a drive on a highway. To clear the way, sometimes you have to overtake others without their permission.

👍 When you are not in a hurry is the best time to show your altruism and courtesy by giving priority for others to pass. This will pay you back very well during your rushed times.

👍 Getting big space at the cost of others won't necessarily help you reach your destination quickly. Just focus on utilizing your dedicated path efficiently.

👍 Regardless of how well you are prepared, you will always be in need of good company.

👍 Stopping to help someone might delay you for a while, but it satisfies an essential spiritual need inside you. And it pays back directly or indirectly.

👍 Before making the decision to neglect anyone on your way, make sure that you have accurately evaluated the consequences of the person's absence.

👍 The harm of a useless person on your way is not limited to wasting your time. The person occupies a space deserved by a better individual.

👍 Being focused should not stop you from keeping your head up and looking around. Just avoid frequently looking behind you.

👍 Observe physical and moral personal space for yourself and others. However, be ready to accept smartly minor overtaking, and be able to deal decisively and wisely with obvious encroachment.

👍 When other people stare at you pointedly, it means either that you are admired by them or they are expressing their resentment. Both assumptions are not supposed to make you angry. Admiring you invites joy and pride. And the way someone expresses discontent through staring reflects his or her passive personality.

WHEN CAN YOU OBTAIN YOUR BEST VERSION?

19

👍 Be careful before being convinced that you have obtained the best copy of yourself. The best of you is not only one final copy; it is a continuous renewal process of self-assessments.

👍 Always consider improving your actions toward getting the best version of yourself. Do not only focus on increasing the number of these actions.

👍 If an action plan lasts for a long time, you probably need to change the plan or perform a reevaluation to scrutinize identified actions or even replace them.

👍 What makes others their best probably won't suit you. Look inside yourself, discover your characteristics, and create your own achievements.

👍 Do not wait for the dreamed best version of yourself to feel confident. Work hard, and always trust the current version of yourself.

👍 Obtaining the best possible copy is not the final stage. If you do not work hard to maintain it, you might lose that copy.

🖒 However, do not worry if you lose control over your best copy and return to a worse version. You can still get the best copy of yourself within that version.

🖒 You might not be able to enhance what you believe is a best version of yourself, but you definitely need to implement the continuously required updates to that version.

🖒 Always remember that the idea behind the saying, "The best version of yourself," is to avoid frequent unnecessary comparisons with others.

🖒 Make sure not to lose even a little bit of complacency as you strive to get the best version of yourself.

🖒 Do not rush. You are getting the best version of yourself out of your worst copy experiences.

DESTINATION

20

👍 When it is not possible to reach your aimed destination as planned by today, it is better to take some steps to help you reach your destination by tomorrow rather than to just wait helplessly.

👍 If all doors to your destination are found closed today, knock on different doors to discover some other areas. This, of course, is better than waiting for your destination's doors to open.

👍 Others will have the chance to set your destination when you hesitate to move or when you rush anywhere without a prior plan.

👍 If you could not achieve your goals, that does not mean your decision to move was wrong. It probably has something to do with the appropriate selection of your destination or the approach you took to reach the selected destination.

👍 Physical destinations are not that difficult to target. Be more careful with and attentive to your moral and spiritual goals.

👍 Unlike sports competitions, the destination of any journey is not a finish line. Most important is what you find and acquire by the end of the journey.

👍 You need to reach your destination fast and safely, but before that, ensure that you achieve your goals. You could reach your destination with many gains taken from you while going down the road.

👍 The outcome at your destination depends in one way or another on how you handle every detail along your way.

👍 As no journey is literally repeated, you cannot reach the same destination twice in life.

👍 We do not make the decision to start every journey in our lives. But we are definitely responsible for shaping the way we reach all our destinations.

👍 When the journey is too long and the destination seems to be difficult to reach, try to refresh and recharge yourself by celebrating your achievements at each milestone.

👍 Never underestimate the significance of the stations along your way by considering the destination as the only target of the journey.

👍 Good planning does not mean that you do not need to revise some of the journey's details on your way.

👍 While on your way, you sometimes have to make an immediate decision about a significant change of the destination itself.

👍 Never regret your decision to go; you either earned or learned something.

👍 To reach the destination faster, safer, and happier, try to enjoy every detail. And do not forget to observe the time allocated to each part of the journey.

👍 The fact that you do not set all your destinations in life should not stop you from determining the path to be taken and the output to deliver at each destination.

👍 To be a pioneer, you do not necessarily need to set a destination that has not been reached by anyone before. You could be a role model by the approach you take to reach any destination.

👍 Whatever the outcomes of the journey, each destination is a starting point for another journey.

Printed in the United States
By Bookmasters